Introduction

Creating beautiful quilts is more than just a craft; it's a journey into a rich tradition passed down through generations. Each stitch holds a connection to the past, honoring the skill, patience, and creativity of those who came before us. The intricate patterns and designs, whether traditional or modern, allow quilters to tell stories, preserve memories, and leave their mark on a living art form. Quilts become tangible embodiments of love, comfort, and shared history, making each stitch a testament to the enduring legacy of this beloved practice.

Table of Contents

Fabric	Threads/Yarn	Needles
Plush, Velvets, and Wools	Silk Ribbon, Silk Buttonhole Twist, Flower Thread, Cotton and Rayon Embroidery Floss	Crewel No. 6-8 or Chenille No. 18-24
Cottons, Polyesters, Linens, and Shantungs	Persian Wool, Pearl Cotton, Tapestry Wool, Metallics, Flower Thread, Cotton and Rayon Embroidery Floss	Crewel No. 4-7 or Tapestry No. 20 or 22
Moiré, Taffeta, and Satins	Brazilian Embroidery Thread, Pearl Cotton, Metallics, Flower Thread, Cotton and Rayon Embroidery Floss	Crewel No. 4-8
Lightweight Silks, Organzas, and Batistes	Brazilian Embroidery Thread, Linen Thread, Pearl Cotton, Metallics, Silk Buttonhole Twist, Flower Thread, Cotton and Rayon Embroidery Floss	Crewel No. 6-8
Loosely Woven Fabrics	Persian Wool and Crewel Yarns	Chenille No. 18 or 20

BASIC STITCHES AND VARIATIONS

BACKSTITCH

Basic

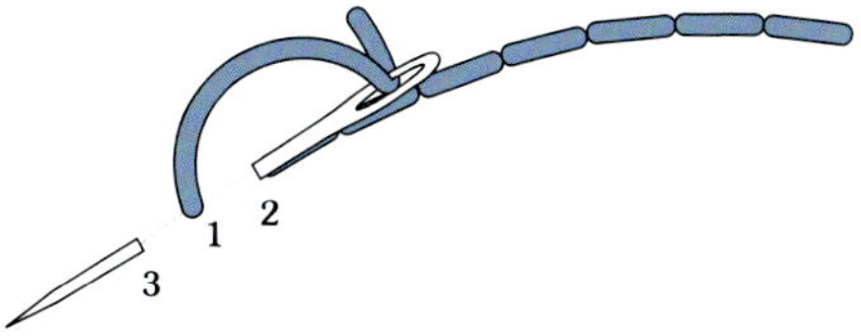

Backstitch — Variation

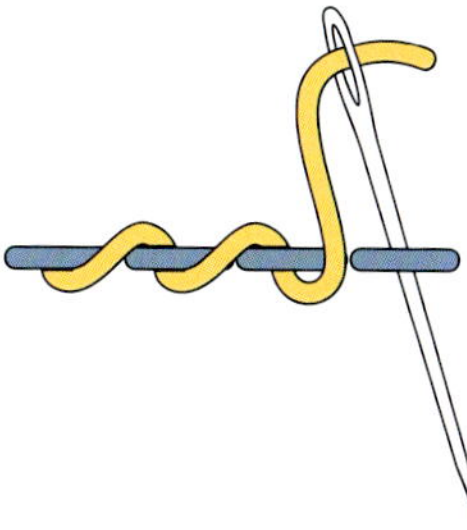

BLANKET

Basic

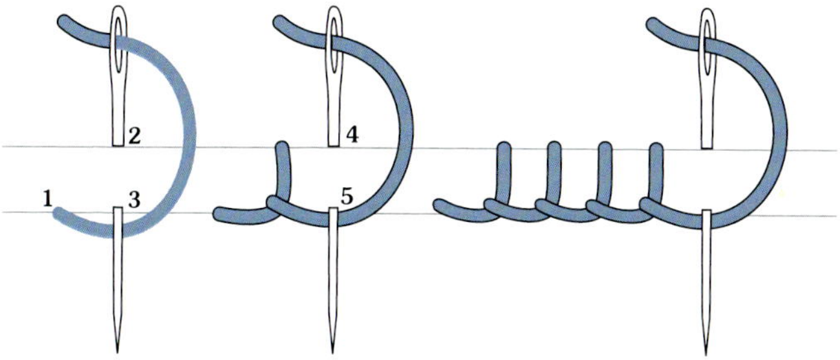

Blanket — Variation A

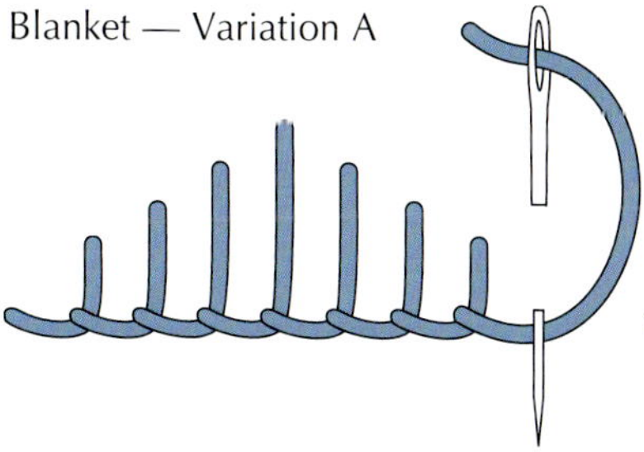

Blanket — Variation B

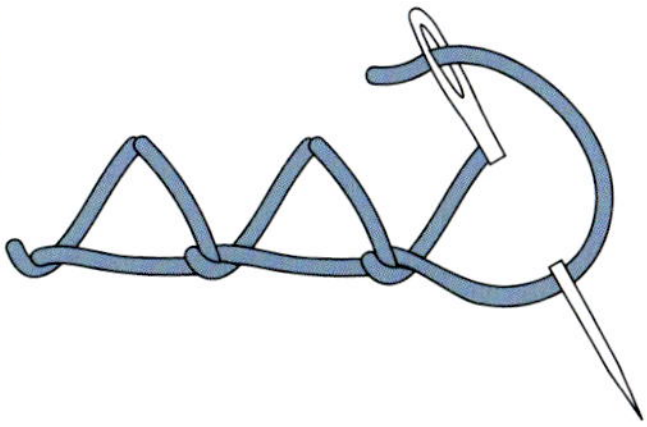

Blanket — Variation C

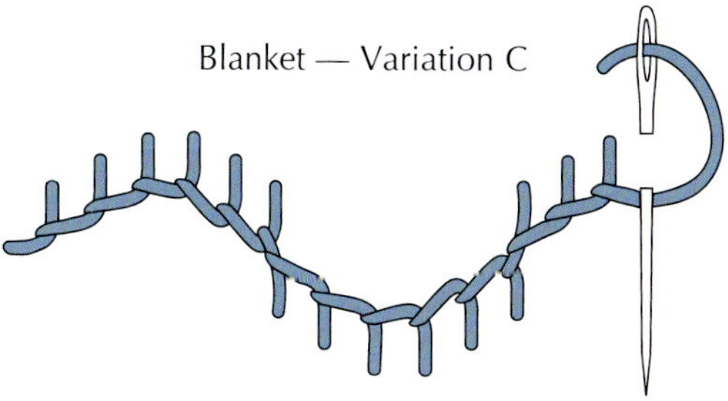

BULLION

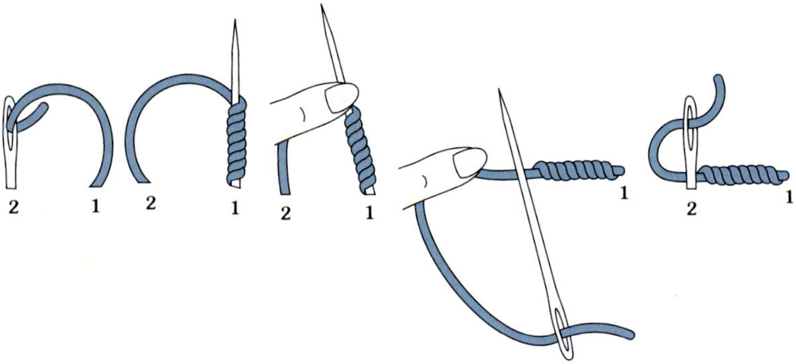

CHAIN

Basic

Chain — Variation

CHEVRON

Basic

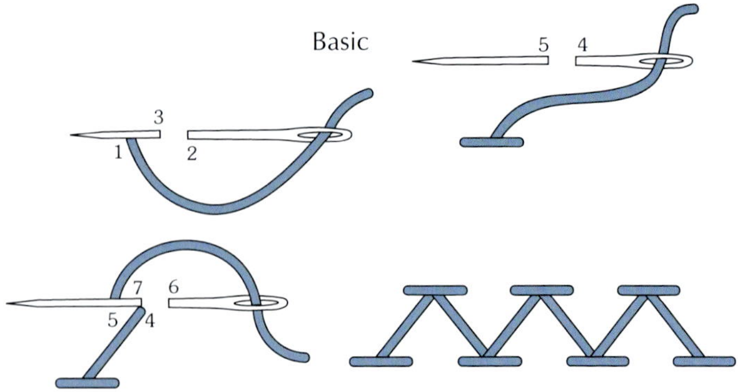

Chevron — Variation

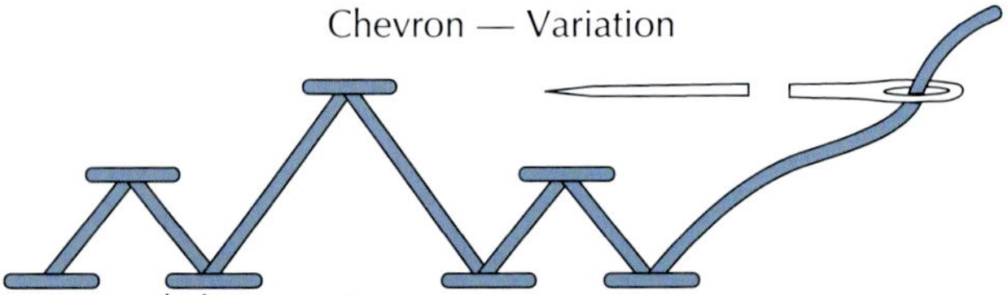

COUCHING

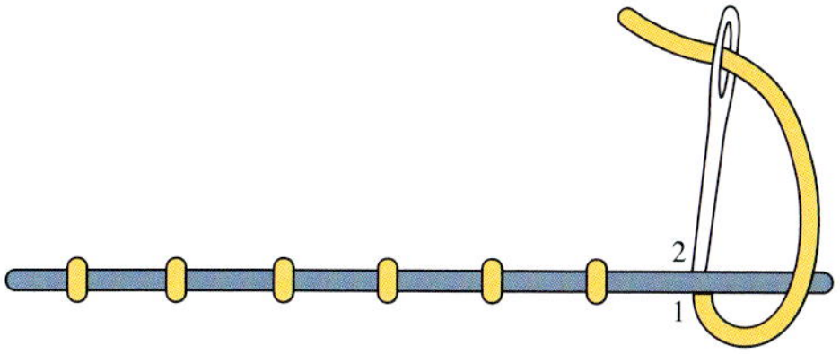

CRETAN

Basic

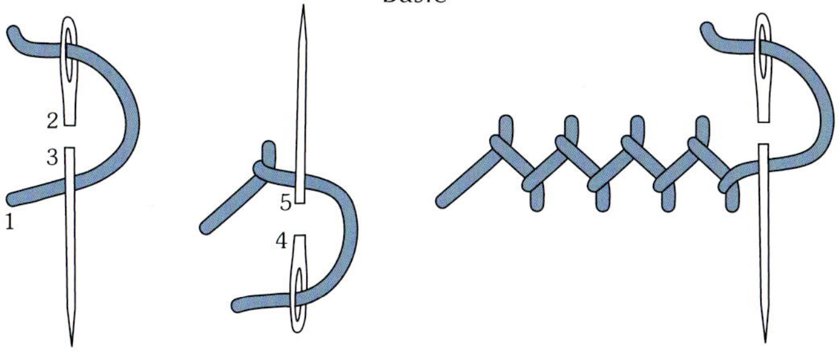

Cretan — Variation

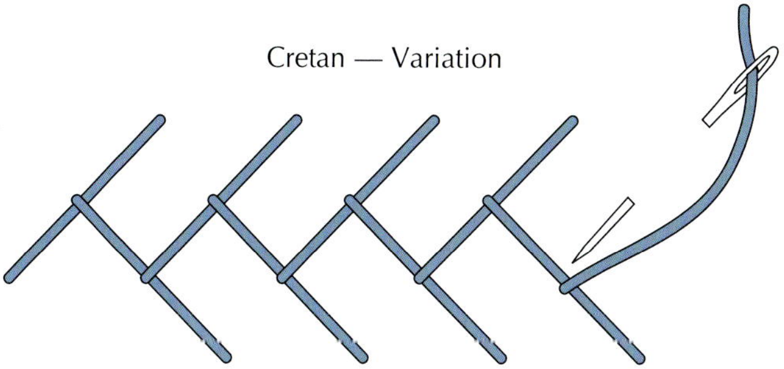

CROSS

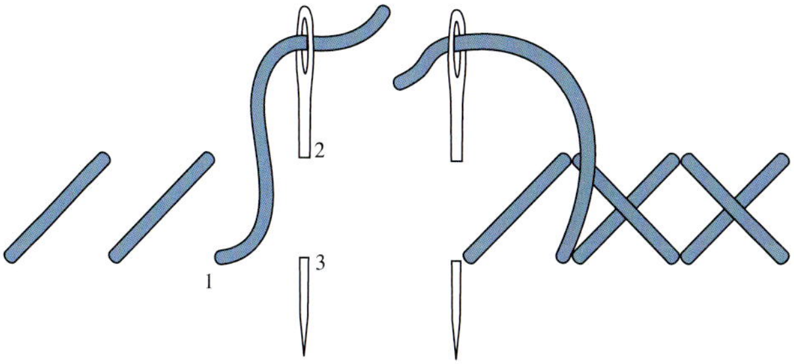

FEATHER

Basic

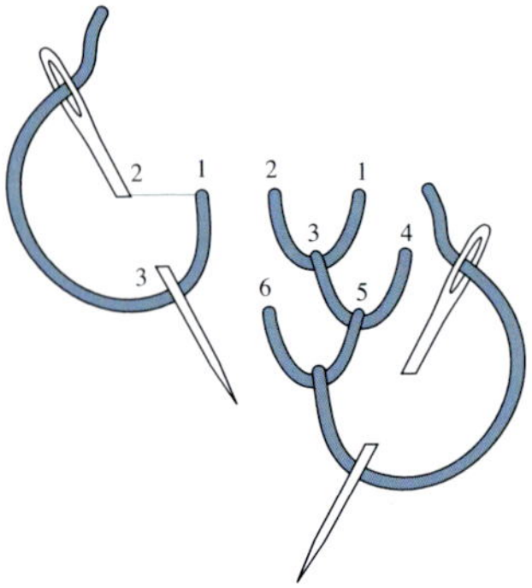

Feather — Variation

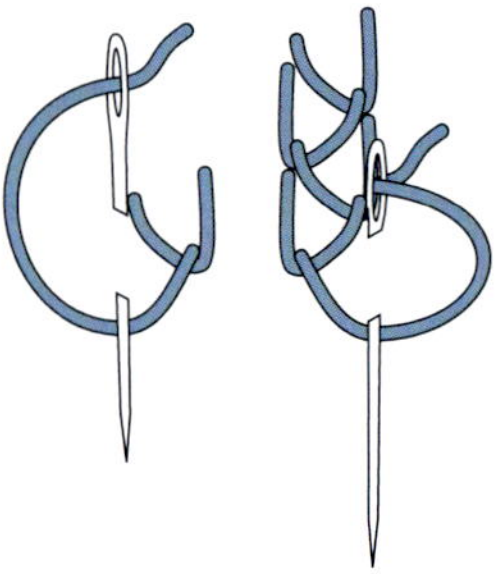

FERN LEAF

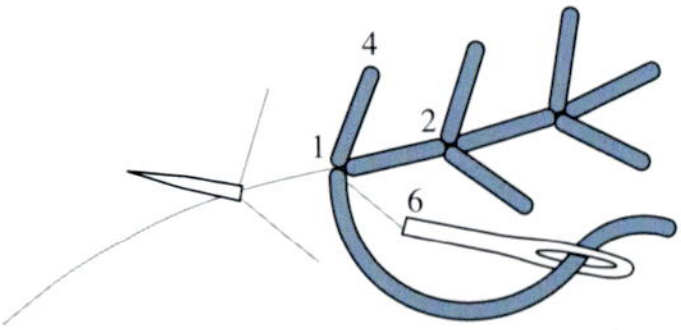

FLY

Basic

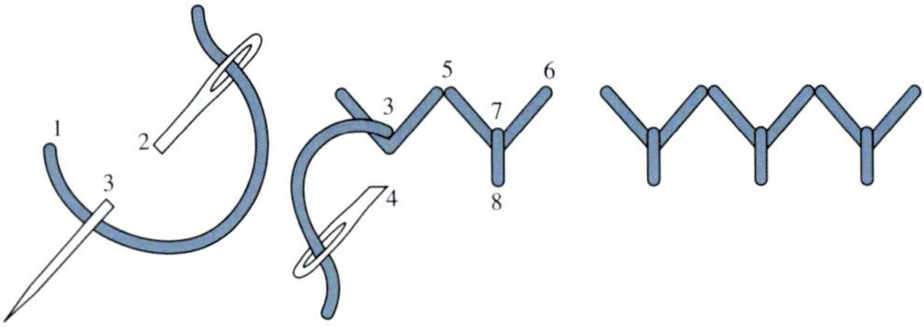

Fly — Variation A

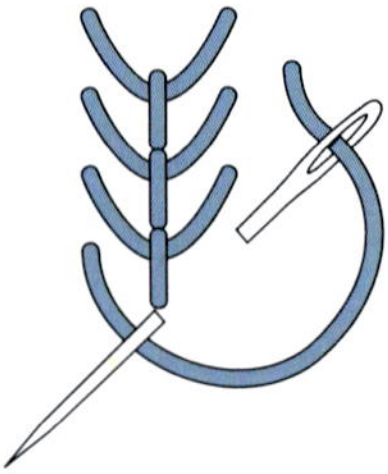

Fly — Variation B

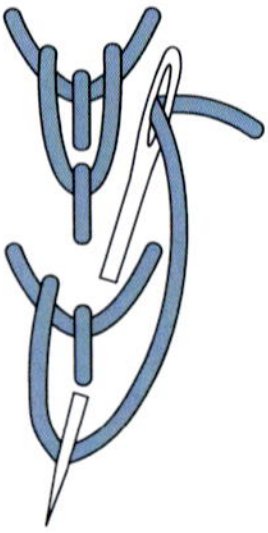

Fly — Variation C

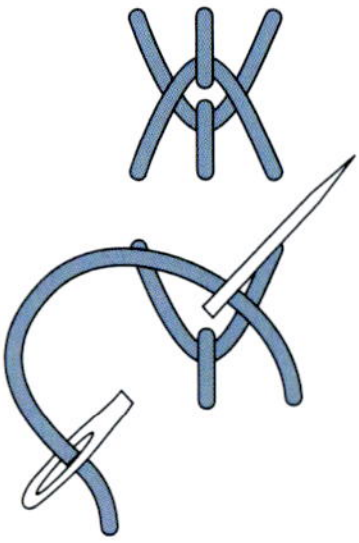

FRENCH KNOT

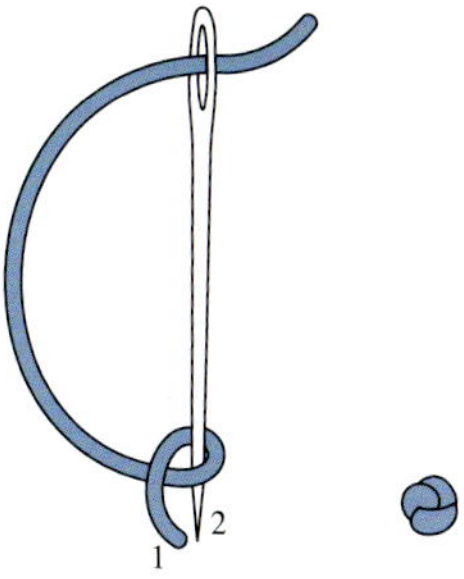

HERRINGBONE

Basic

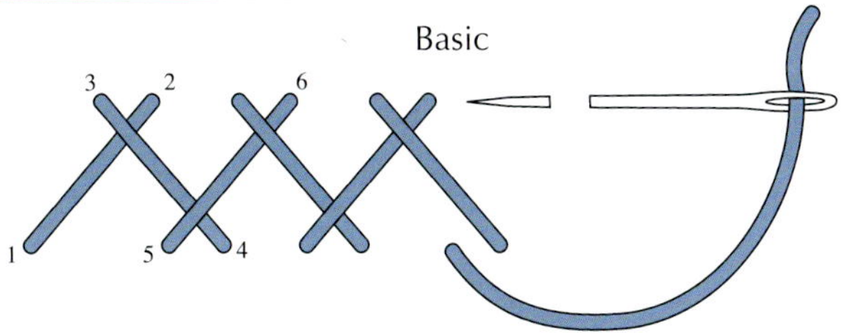

Herringbone — Variation

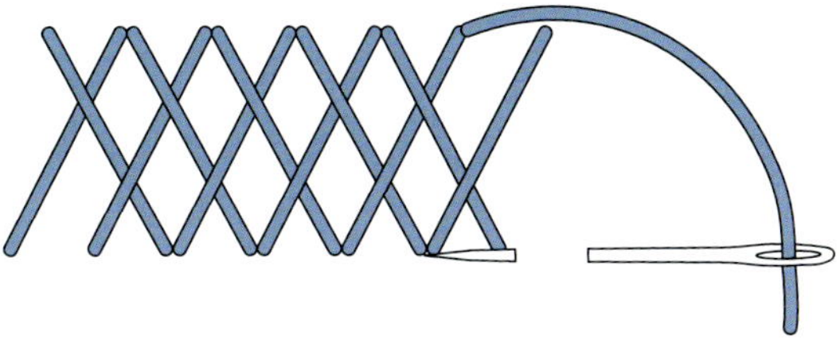

LAZY DAISY

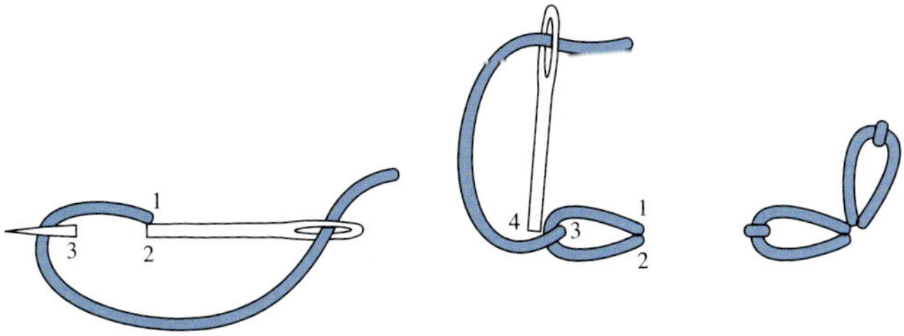

PISTIL

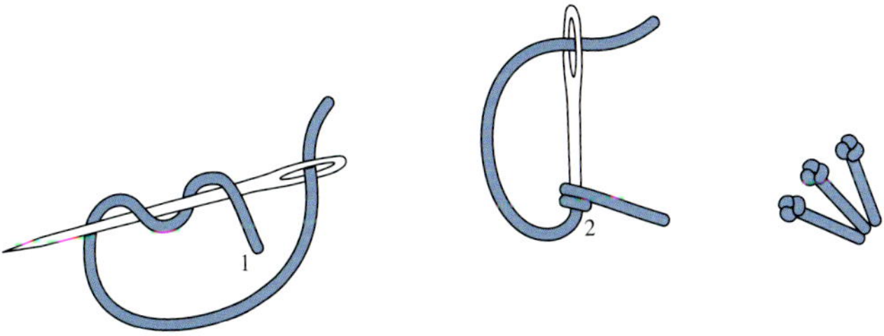

RUNNING

Basic

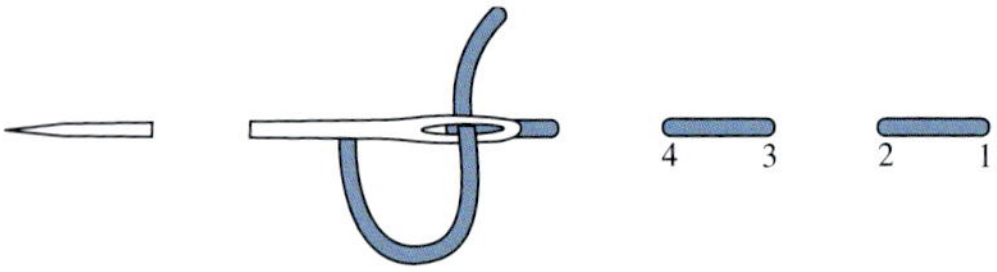

Running — Variation A

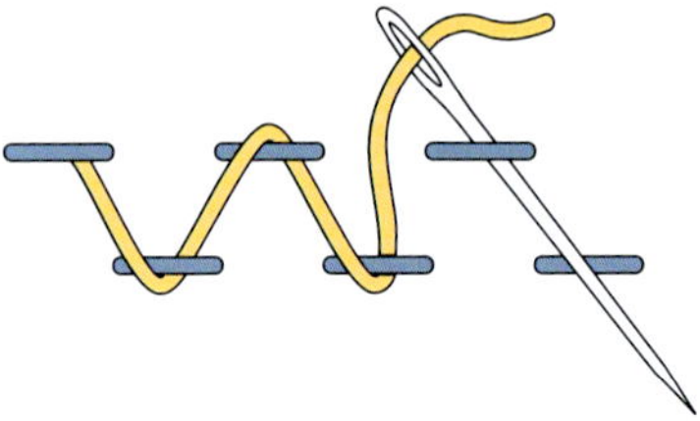

Running — Variation B

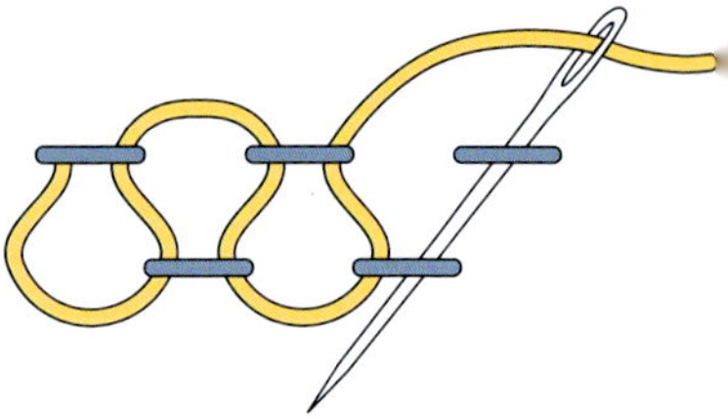

SHEAF

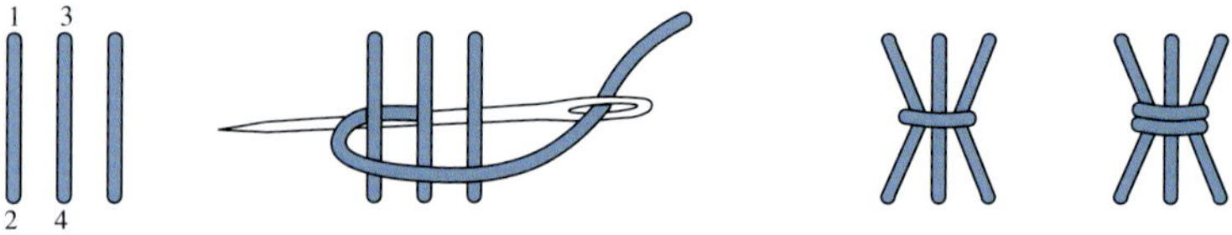

STEM

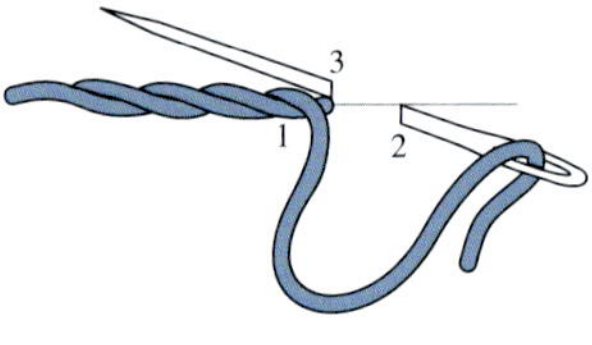

STRAIGHT

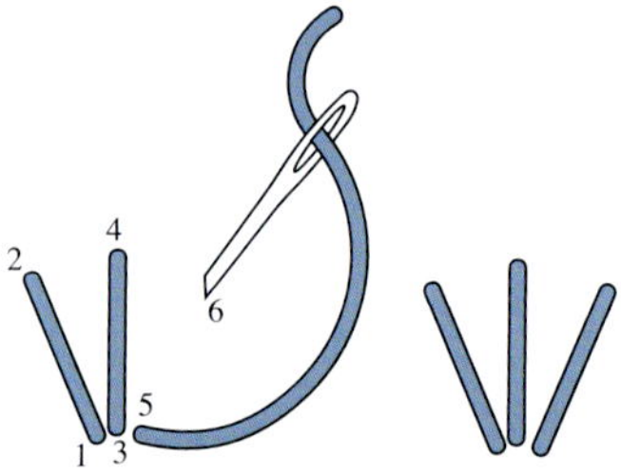

COMBINATION STITCHES

For clarity, each stitch within one combination is shown in a different color.

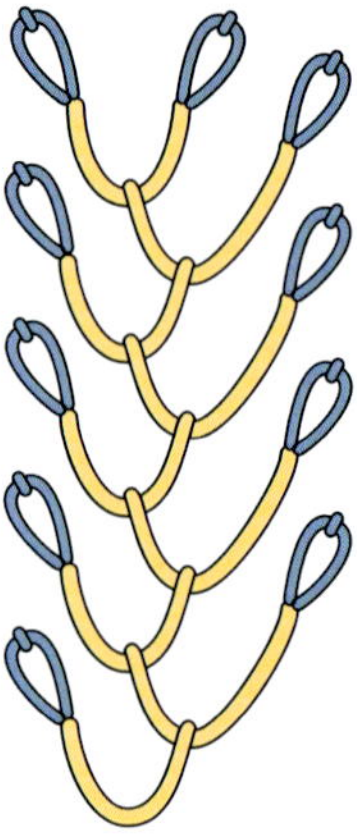

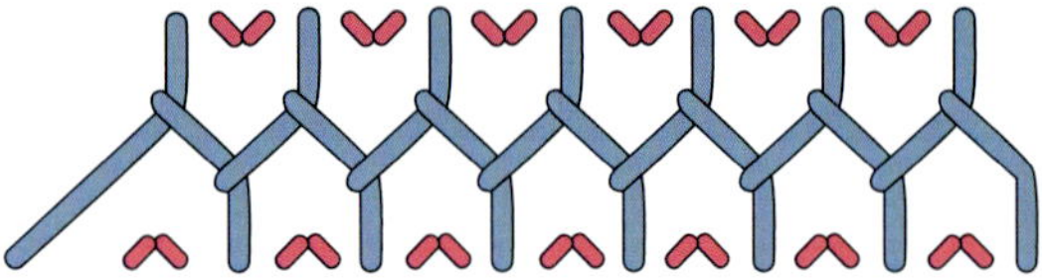

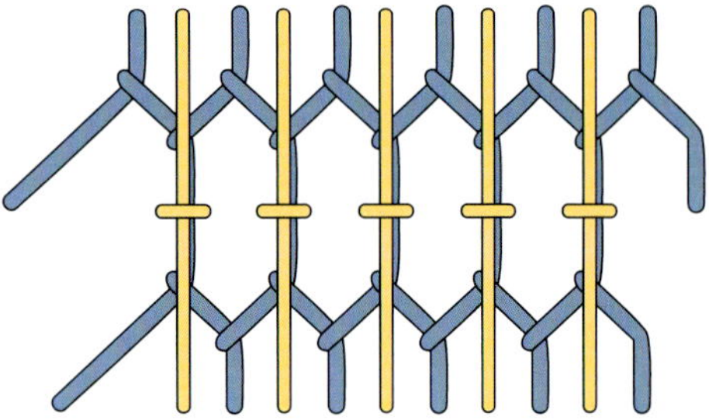

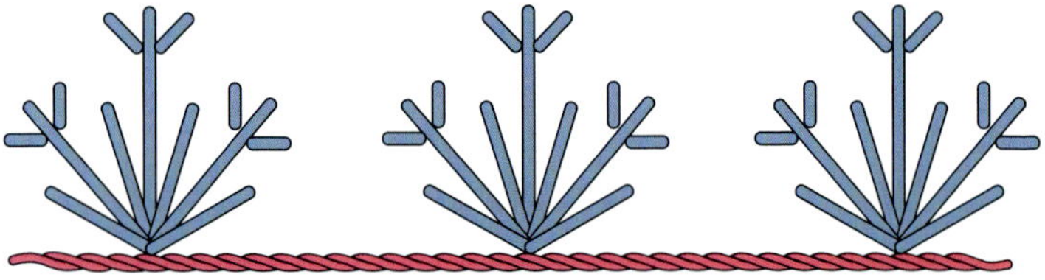

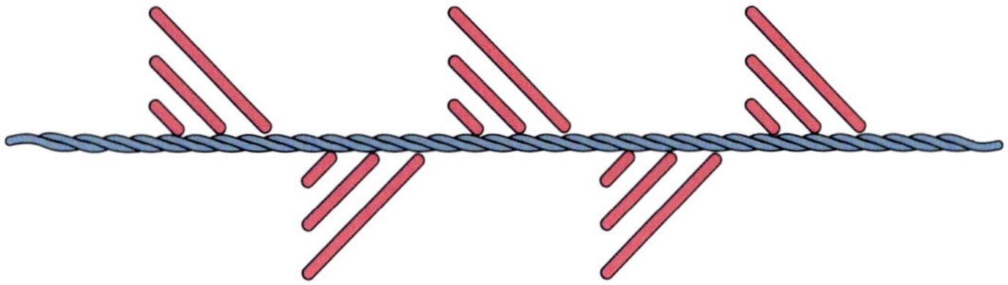

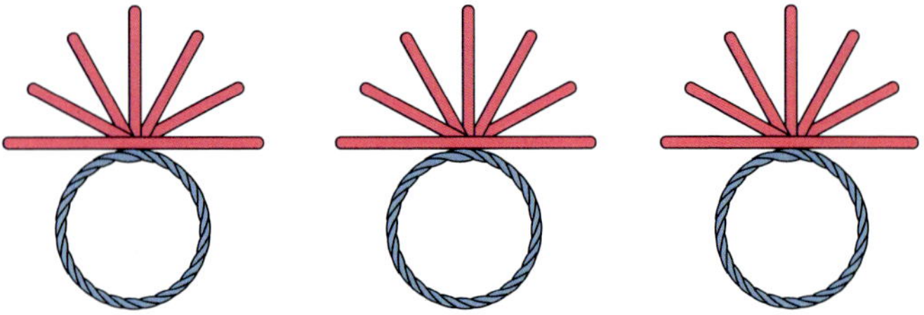

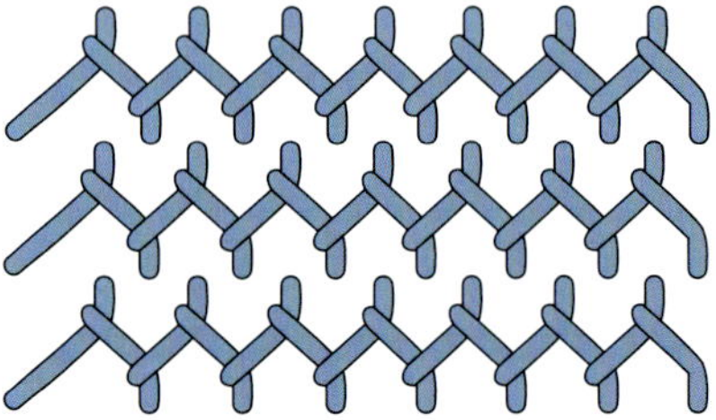

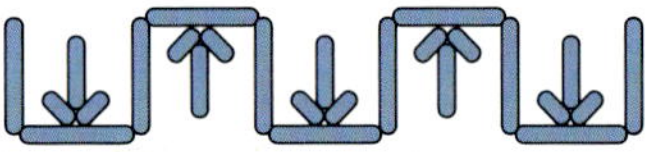

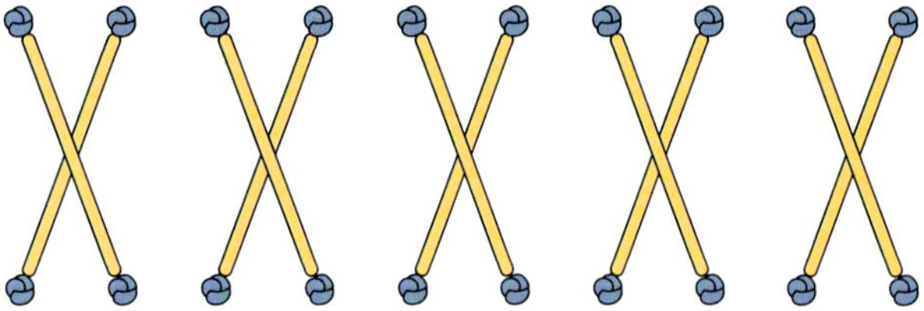

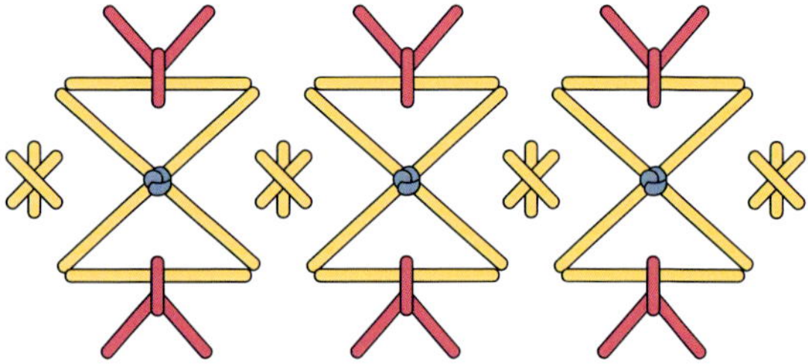

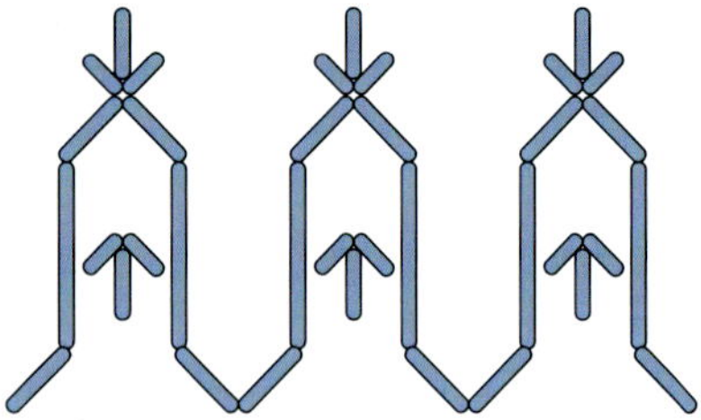

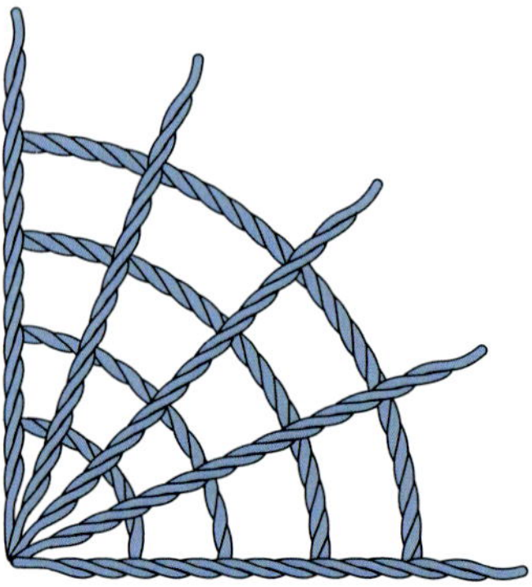

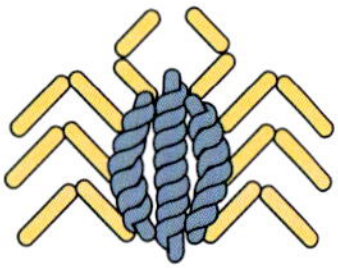